MW00737832

entering
God's
presence

Other Studies in A Mom's Ordinary Day Bible Study Series

Jean E. Syswerda is mother to three grown children. A former editor and associate publisher at Zondervan, she was responsible for such best-selling Bibles as the *NIV Adventure Bible,* the *NIV Teen Study Bible,* and the *NIV Women's Devotional Bible 1.* She is the general editor of the *NIV Women of Faith Study Bible* and the *NLT Prayer Bible,* as well as the coauthor of the *Read with Me Bible* and the best-selling *Women of the Bible.*

Natalie J. Block is a freelance writer and Bible editor living in Belmont, Michigan. She is the author of the fifty-two "Enjoying God" Bible studies in the *NIV Women of Faith Study Bible.* Natalie and her husband, Greg, share a passion for prayer and together they direct their church's prayer ministry.

six sessions

YOU & GOD . YOU & OTHERS . YOU & YOUR KIDS

mom

a mom's ordinary day

BIBLE STUDY SERIES

entering
God's
presence

**JEAN E.
SYSWERDA**

general editor

written by
**NATALIE J.
BLOCK**

ZONDERVAN™

GRAND RAPIDS, MICHIGAN 49530 USA

We want to hear from you. Please send your comments about this book to us in care of zreview@zondervan.com. Thank you.

ZONDERVAN™

Entering God's Presence
Copyright © 2003 by Jean Syswerda

Requests for information should be addressed to:

Zondervan, *Grand Rapids, Michigan 49530*

ISBN 0-310-24718-7

All Scripture quotations, unless otherwise indicated, are taken from the *Holy Bible: New International Version®*. NIV®. Copyright © 1973, 1978, 1984 by International Bible Society. Used by permission of Zondervan. All rights reserved.

All rights reserved. No part of this publication may be reproduced, stored in a retrieval system, or transmitted in any form or by any means—electronic, mechanical, photocopy, recording, or any other—except for brief quotations in printed reviews, without the prior permission of the publisher.

Interior design by Tracey Moran

Printed in the United States of America

03 04 05 06 07 08 09 /❖ CH/ 10 9 8 7 6 5 4 3 2 1

contents

how to use this study guide

Hey, Mom, are you ready?

When was the last time you did something just for you?

In the joy and junk and memories and mess that is your life as a mother, do you sometimes feel that you've lost something—something essential and important?

The Bible studies in this series will help you rediscover and, even more, enjoy all the parts and pieces that make you a unique person, a unique mother, and a unique and holy creation of God.

The five sections of each individual session are designed to meet a particular need in your life—the need for time alone, for time with God's Word, for time with others, for time with God, and for time with your children. How you approach and use each section is up to you and your individual styles and desires. But here are a few suggestions:

For You Alone

The operative word here is, of course, *alone.* For moms who rarely even go to the bathroom alone, being alone can seem an almost impossible goal. Perhaps thinking in terms of *quiet* would help. You can do this part of the study in any quiet moments in your home—when kids are sleeping, when they're watching a video, when you're nursing a little one. Any quiet or personal time you can find in your own schedule will work. This part of the study is sometimes serious, sometimes fun, sometimes downright silly. It will prepare your mind for the other sections of the study.

For You and God's Word

Put this study guide, a pen, and your Bible in a favorite place—somewhere you can grab it at any free moment, perhaps in the kitchen or by a favorite chair. Then, when a few spare moments arise, everything you need is right at hand. Each of the six sessions includes a short Bible study for you to complete alone. (This doesn't necessarily mean you have to *be* alone to complete it! My daughter reads her Bible out loud during a morning bath while her infant son sits in his bouncy seat next to her. She gets her Bible read, and he's content with the sound of his mommy's voice.)

For You and Others

The third section of each study is intended for small groups (even just two is a small group!), but if that isn't possible, you *can* complete it alone. Or connect with a friend or neighbor to work through the materials together. If you function as the leader, little preparation is required; you can learn right along with your fellow mothers. The leader is actually more of a facilitator, keeping the discussion on track and your time together moving along. Leadership information on many of the questions in the "For You and Others" section is included at the back of this book, beginning on page 75.

For You and God

The fourth section of each session will guide you in a time of prayer based on the study's topic. Wonder when you'll find time to do this? Prop this book up in your window while doing dishes. God hears the prayers of moms whose hands are in dishwater! Or take it along in the car when picking up a child from an activity. Or use it while nursing an infant. These times of talking to God are precious moments in the life of a mom. And with all the demands on your time, you need to grab these moments whenever you can. Do also try, though, to find a time each day for quiet, concentrated prayer. Your children need their mom to be "prayed up" when she faces each day.

For You and Your Kids

How great is this? A Bible study that includes something for your kids as well as for you! The final section of each session gives suggestions on applying the principles of the study in your kids' lives as well as in your own. The activities are appropriately geared to different ages and range from simple to more complex.

One Important Final Note

Don't presume you have to move through these sessions in any particular order. The order in which they appear in each study is the ideal. Life doesn't always allow the ideal, however. If you start your study with the last section and then go through from back to front, you'll still be fine. Do whatever works best for you and your schedule and for your treasured little (or not-so-little) offspring.

introduction

Prayer is both incredibly simple and unimaginably complicated.

- How can a five-year-old child have a more powerful prayer life than an adult?

- Why do answers to some prayers come quickly, while answers to others are slow in coming or seem never to come at all?

- Why does God answer an "impossible" request but apparently ignore an "easy" one?

These are questions you've asked yourself. Although it's true that there are things about prayer that are a mystery, the Bible has a lot to say about prayer. This study will teach you how to make prayer a powerful, rewarding, and energizing part of your Christian walk.

As a mom, you're bombarded with an unending list of things to do. Do you have time for a prayer life? Is it really that important? Can it really make a difference?

Yes, yes, yes! You may find that God speaks most clearly to you in the laundry room while you're folding clothes. You may suddenly find that you love being part of the car pool, because the car has become your "prayer closet" after you drop off the kids. And you may discover that Jesus is even more faithful, loving, and wonderful than you ever imagined.

As you work through this study, you'll discover that God is always available to you, that intimacy with him brings passion to prayer, and that you need only a small faith to move the mountains in your life. You will learn the "conditions" that sometimes have to be met for prayers to be answered, the things that can block answers to prayer, and effective ways to intercede for your husband, children, and friends. You will dig deep within yourself to discover how you can be deceived and how your mind can be used by Satan to prevent you from believing the truth about who you are and understanding the power you possess in prayer. And you will discover ways to determine what God's will is, so you can pray with the confidence that God hears you and that you have what you ask of him.

Whew! That's a lot of ground to cover. This study may be a challenge for you. It's a journey that may require hard work on your part, but keep *the goal* in mind. You will reap the benefits a thousand times over. So dig in! God has a wonderful, life-changing plan in store for you—and you don't want to miss it!

welcome to the throne room

For You Alone

When you hear the word *prayer,* what comes to your mind? Check all the boxes that apply.

❑ boring	❑ calming
❑ a last resort	❑ time-consuming
❑ not my thing	❑ difficult
❑ a psychological exercise	❑ a wish list
❑ fun	❑ a waste of time
❑ a stress reliever	❑ refreshing
❑ conversation	❑ rewarding
❑ for the spiritually elite	❑ frustrating
❑ sleep-inducing	❑ a mealtime requirement

Prayer is often defined as "a conversation with God." And so it is, but it's also much more. Prayer is the spiritual *union* of the believer with God. In prayer you acknowledge who God is and who you are. Through prayer you experience God's presence, God's forgiveness, and the release of God's power, which enables you to do his will in your life and in his world. Prayer is action. Prayer is the secret to a powerful and rewarding Christian life.

> *Carry on an ongoing conversation with God about the daily stuff of life.... Do not worry about "proper" praying, just talk to God. Share your hurts, share your sorrows. Share your joys—freely and openly.... When we do this, we will discover something of inestimable value. We will discover that by praying we learn to pray.*
>
> RICHARD FOSTER, *PRAYER*

 ## For You and God's Word

Read Ephesians 2:1 – 10. As you read, take the "you" in this passage personally. Recognize who you were and who you now are. Satan does not want you to discover who you are. He wants you to think you're still the person you used to be. He wants you to believe that you are powerless and alone—but these verses reveal something very different.

1. What was your former condition (verse 1)? Note the use of the past tense in verses 1 and 2. What kind of lifestyle did you lead in your former condition (verse 3)?

2. What is your present condition (verse 5)?

3. What changes have occurred in your life because of this change in your condition?

4. What motivated God to change your condition (verse 4)?

5. What is your present spiritual position in Christ, that is, where are you seated spiritually (verse 6)?

6. What was God's purpose in raising you to this position (verse 7)?

7. How did you get into this new position in Christ (verse 8)?

8. What purpose does God have for you now (verse 10)?

9. Is this a new concept for you? If this truth were to penetrate your heart, how would it affect your prayer life?

10. List three practical, everyday ways you can respond to God in gratitude for your new position with Christ.

What marvelous love God has for you! Not only has he saved you, making you alive in Christ, but he has also spiritually seated you by his side in heaven, giving you immediate and continual access to him through prayer. God is always available to you. So, come on. Welcome to the throne room.

> *You complain that it is hard for you to pray, to experience the love of Jesus.... Where you are most human, most yourself, weakest, there Jesus lives. Bringing your fearful self home is bringing Jesus home.*
>
> HENRI NOUWEN, *THE INNER VOICE OF LOVE*

For You and Others

As a believer, you are "raised" with Christ and "seated" with God (Ephesians 2:6), right in the throne room, which gives you incredible access to the Father. Why? Why would God put you there? As a group, read Hebrews 10:19–25 to discover the reason.

1. What does "the Most Holy Place" in verse 19 refer to (see also Hebrews 9:24)?

2. In Old Testament times, God's people had access to him through the high priest. Who is your "great priest" (verse 21), and when did he enter the Most Holy Place (Acts 1:9–11; Hebrews 4:14)?

3. What makes it possible for you to come into God's presence (verses 19–21)?

4. How should you approach God in prayer (verses 19, 22)? How should this attitude affect your prayer life in a practical way?

Through his death, resurrection, and ascension, Jesus, your high priest, has opened the way for you to personally come into God's presence. The "curtain" (verse 20) that once blocked the Most Holy Place (Exodus 26:31–33) was permanently torn, or "opened" (verse 20), when Jesus died (Matthew 27:51). You now have direct access to God.

5. What should you do now that you have this access to God (verse 22)?

6. According to verse 22, the best environment for drawing near to God comprises four parts. See if you can list each part and tell its key role in a fruitful prayer life:

Part 1 (1 Chronicles 29:17; Job 33:3):

_____

Part 2 (Matthew 17:20; Hebrews 11:6; James 1:5–8):

_____

Part 3 (Psalm 32:5; Isaiah 59:2):

_____

Part 4 (Exodus 29:4; Ezekiel 36:24–29; Ephesians 5:26):

_____

7. Why can you come to God with a sense of hope (verse 23)?

8. What does God's faithfulness mean to you personally? Do you have trouble accepting the fact that God is faithful and trustworthy? Why or why not?

9. What should drawing near to God inspire you to do (verses 24–25)?

10. What practical things could you do to encourage your husband and your children to draw near to God and to express their love through good deeds? How can you do the same for your friends?

The most important and satisfying relationship you can ever have is the one you have with God. When your desire for God becomes a *longing,* you will begin to draw near to him in prayer.

11. When you draw near to God in prayer, what does he promise to do (James 4:8)?

12. What do these verses tell you are the results of an active and intimate prayer life?

2 Corinthians 3:18 _____

Philippians 3:10 _____

Colossians 2:2 – 3 _____

2 Peter 1:3 _____

 ## For You and God

Drawing near to God is an incredible privilege. It is humbling to come before the Creator of the universe, the One who knows everything about you. But you can be assured of his love for you and his deep desire for intimacy with you.

Ephesians 1:3 says, "Praise be to the God and Father of our Lord Jesus Christ, who has blessed us in the heavenly realms with every spiritual blessing in Christ." You are not only spiritually seated with Christ in the heavenly realms (Ephesians 2:6), but you have also been blessed with "every spiritual blessing in Christ." Praise God!

Although finding a quiet place can be difficult for a mom, try to take four or five minutes to spend with God in stillness. Words aren't necessary. Simply quiet yourself and think about this awesome God who loves you. Let your thoughts linger on his goodness to you.

Now express your love for him in a short prayer. Your simple expression of love and praise will delight the Lord.

> *Prayer is the very life of oneness, of being one with Christ.*
> *Therefore prayer is as necessary as the air,*
> *as the blood in our body, as anything, to keep us alive*
> *to the grace of God. To pray generously is not enough,*
> *we must pray devoutly, with fervor and piety.*
> *We must pray perseveringly and with great love.*
> *If we don't pray, our presence will have no power,*
> *our words will have no power.*
>
> MOTHER TERESA, *No Greater Love*

For You and Your Kids

Preschool–Elementary

As you play a game together this week, tell your kids how happy you are when they spend time with you. Tell them that it also makes God happy when they spend time with him. Pray with them a simple prayer: *Dear God, thank you for loving me. Thank you for liking me so much that you can hardly wait to spend time with me. Amen.*

Middle–High School

Ask your kids to name their favorite friend. Do they trust this person enough to tell him or her something very private? Explain that they can bring anything and everything to God, even things they wouldn't tell you or their friends. God will never let them down. Encourage them to spend private time in prayer and build a relationship with God.

All Ages

Assure your kids that nothing is too small to bring to God. He cares about everything in their lives. Because God knows everything, they can tell him even those things they wouldn't dare share with other people. God is faithful, and he will reward their honesty.

where's the passion?

 ## For You Alone

Having a close friend can make life a lot easier—and a lot more fun. Think about your dearest friend. How long did it take for the two of you to become great friends? List four or five things you and your friend did together to develop your relationship:

As you look over your list, you probably notice a few common elements: time together, honesty, trust, loyalty, and communication. These same elements are necessary for building a relationship with God. Now list four or five things you can do to build your relationship with God:

Which of the two lists looks more exciting? Does your second list look, well, boring? Do reading the Bible and praying seem like too much trouble for too little return? As a mom, you may feel that everyone wants a piece of you, that there's just not enough of you left over for another relationship that will take time and energy. Well, here's a surprise: This is a relationship that will just keep on giving—not taking. So set your hopes high for this session. You're about to find out where the passion is.

For You and God's Word

Psalm 63:1–8 is a beautiful expression of the heart's longing for God. Read this passage and answer the following questions. (It's a long list of questions, but as you work through them, you'll discover David's exciting passion for God—and perhaps develop your own.)

1. Desire is essential for a healthy relationship to flourish. How does David describe his desire for God (verse 1)?

    How would you describe your desire (or lack of desire) for God?

    What are some things you can do to increase your desire for God? What are some things you currently do that may be hindering your passion for God?

2. Memories of past experiences can bond people together. What past experiences bonded David with God (verse 2)?

What past experience with God has helped to bond you to him?

3. What was the foundation of David's relationship with God (verse 3)?

Do you ever question God's love for you? Sometimes it is easier for believers to accept God's salvation than to accept the love that motivated it. How can you be reassured of God's love for you?

4. What priority did David's relationship with God have in his life (verse 3)?

What priority does your relationship with God have in your life? How can you make your relationship with God a higher priority?

5. What was David's response to God's love (verse 4)?

What is your response to God's love for you?

6. How did David describe the fulfillment he had found in his relationship with God (verse 5)?

Describe the fulfillment you have (or you wish you had) in your relationship with God.

7. What practice had David developed that fed his passion for God (verse 6)?

List some things you've done that have helped build your relationship with God.

8. Showing appreciation is important in a relationship. How did David express his thanks to God (verse 7)? Did he offer his praise from near or far? What does this say about his relationship with God?

9. A relationship won't survive without commitment. How does verse 8 describe David's commitment to God and God's commitment to David?

How would you describe your commitment to God? God's commitment to you?

Since passion can be fanned into flame or neglected until it dies out, your attention to your relationship with God is critical. A passionate relationship with God leads to a passionate prayer life.

For You and Others

An intimate and passionate relationship with God is the key to an effective and passionate prayer life. To learn more about how to develop your relationship with God, read John 15:1–17 together and answer the following questions.

1. Verses 1–4 express the importance of your relationship with God. In order for your relationship with God to be solid, what do you need to do (verse 4)? List two or three practical things you can do to accomplish this.

2. Verses 5–6 express the vitality of your relationship with God. What will you produce if you "remain" in Christ (verse 5)? List two or three examples of fruit you personally might produce.

3. Verses 7–8 set forth the assurance of your relationship with God. What two conditions must be met in order for your prayers to be answered (verse 7)?

4. Explain what you think the phrases "remain in me" and "remain in you" mean (verse 7).

5. Do you really think God will give you whatever you ask? Explain your answer, noting the "if" condition in verse 7.

6. What does verse 8 describe as the purpose of prayer?

7. Verses 9–12 describe the foundation of your relationship with God. To what is Jesus' love for you compared (verse 9)?

8. Jesus' command is that you remain in his love (verse 9). How do you do that (verse 10)?

9. What will your obedience produce in you (verse 11) and how will it be evident in your life? What could cause it to be *more* in evidence in your life?

10. Verses 13–17 describe the results of your relationship with God. What event was Jesus referring to in verse 13?

11. When you obey God, how is your relationship with God redefined (verses 14–15)?

How are your relationships with other people redefined (verses 12, 17)?

12. In verse 16 the promise of answered prayer is again conditional, but here (as compared with verse 7) the requirement is different. What is it?

13. According to verse 17, what command are you to obey?

See? It all begins with passion—falling in love with Jesus, the One who delights in you. When you begin to believe and experience God's love for you, your love for God and for others will grow. And out of your passion for God and your passion for others will develop a passion for prayer.

For You and God

When you love someone, you want to please that person. It isn't a chore or a hardship to do things you know will bring happiness to your loved one. And it is certainly not hard to feel loving toward someone who delights in you.

> The LORD your God is with you,
>   he is mighty to save.
> He will take great delight in you,
>   he will quiet you with his love,
>   he will rejoice over you with singing.
>
> ZEPHANIAH 3:17

This is the God who loves you!

As you pray today, dwell on God's love for you. Find one Scripture verse each day in the next week that expresses God's love for you. (You can select passages from a subject index or a concordance in the back of most Bibles.) Meditate on these truths throughout the week.

Where's the passion? It's overflowing from God toward you. As you accept his love, your passion for him will grow and will then flow out into love for others—which will translate into obedience and answered prayer.

For You and Your Kids

Preschool–Elementary

For a fun activity in the car—Warning! This may turn silly—make up your own lyrics to a simple tune (such as "Twinkle, Twinkle, Little Star") that expresses your love for your child. For example, "Mom and Daddy love you so, more than you will ever know. . . ." Encourage your kids to help with the lyrics. The sillier you get with the lyrics, the sillier your kids will get, until smiles and laughter radiate throughout the car and communicate as much as the lyrics of the song. Explain to your children that God has the same sense of delight in them and love for them.

Middle–High School

Remind your kids of your earlier discussion regarding their favorite friend (page 22). Ask them to list some things they did with their friend to develop their friendship. Explain that their relationship with God requires the same kind of time, commitment, trust, and communication. To ensure that they are building a strong relationship with God, encourage them to spend time each day reading the Bible and praying.

All Ages

Explain to your kids that love is expressed through obedience. As love for God grows, so will obedience. They can evaluate their relationship with God by asking themselves the following question: Am I doing things that please God?

where's the power?

 For You Alone

When it comes to power and authority, most moms feel as though they're at the bottom of the "power ladder." When you think about spiritual power, do you feel that you're the last person God would use to do something miraculous? You might be surprised at the amount of power you possess.

Power has several definitions. For purposes of this session, we'll define *power* as the "ability to act" *(Webster's)* and *authority* as the "freedom" or "right" *(Webster's)* to exercise power. For example, you have the power (ability) to drive through every red light you approach, but you don't exercise this power because you don't have the authority (freedom or right) to do so. And although police have the power (ability) and authority (freedom or right) to drive through red lights, they don't exercise their power to do so on a whim. They have permission to use their power and authority only when on official police business.

In this session you will discover the truth about the incredible power, authority, and permission that God has given you. To begin, list three things (we'll call them "mountains" later) in your life that you would change if you had the power *and* the authority to do so.

_____

_____

_____

For You and God's Word

Read John 14:11–14, then answer the following questions to discover where power in prayer can be found.

1. Jesus told his followers that they would do "even greater things than these" (verse 12). What "things" was Jesus referring to (verse 11)?

    What was the condition for doing these "greater things" (verse 12)?

2. Write out the first sentence of verse 12. (You'll be amazed at how much more attention you give and how much more you remember if you write down a verse.) What word is used to describe those who will do what Jesus did if they have faith? Does this mean *you?*

3. What do you think it means to have faith in Jesus?

4. What difference would it make that Jesus was going to the Father (John 14:25–26; 15:26)?

5. How is the gift of the Holy Spirit the key to doing "greater things" (Acts 1:8; 1 John 4:4)?

6. How does the Spirit's power help you in prayer (Romans 8:26–27)?

7. Describe a time when you didn't know what to pray. What happened? How did the Holy Spirit help you (or how could he have helped you)?

8. What things will Jesus do if you ask him in his name (verse 13)?

9. What does "anything" mean in verse 14 (compare 1 John 5:14)? What confidence does this give you in your prayer life?

How can you develop the faith to ask for "anything" and expect to receive it?

You have been given the power you need through the Holy Spirit (Acts 1:8). Jesus has delegated his authority to you as his disciple (Matthew 28:18–20) through faith in him (John 14:12). And he has given you permission to use that power "in [his] name" (John 14:14), when you pray according to God's will (1 John 5:14).

If you desire a more powerful prayer life, ask for the filling of the Holy Spirit; he is Christ's power "at work within [you]" (Ephesians 3:20). Ask the Father to increase your faith, for faith is both a gift and a seed that grows to maturity. Finally, ask the Father to show you his will, so that you can pray with power "in Jesus' name."

For You and Others

Read Mark 11:22-26 together and then answer the following questions.

1. How would you define faith? The Bible's definition can be found in Hebrews 11:1. Look at it, but write your own personal definition here.

2. The opposite of faith is doubt (verse 23). Why is doubt so destructive (James 1:6-8)?

3. How does Satan use doubt to undermine a powerful prayer life?

4. What are some practical ways you can build your faith?

5. What "mountains" (obstacles) do you face? Recall the things you listed at the end of the "For You Alone" section. Add any others that come to mind right now. Are they emotional? Relational? Physical? Spiritual? How can faith move them?

6. What do you do with those obstacles, prayed about in faith, that you *know* Jesus can change or overcome, but he doesn't?

7. Notice that Jesus told his disciples to *say* something to the mountain — to command it to move. How is "speaking" (action) connected to "believing" (faith)? (See Romans 10:10; James 2:17, 22.)

8. What has Jesus promised to do in response to faith combined with action (verse 24)?

9. In verse 25, Jesus connected receiving answers to prayer with a condition. What is that condition?

10. How can Satan use an unwillingness to forgive to undermine a powerful and effective prayer life (2 Corinthians 2:10–11)?

11. How far must you go in forgiving others (Matthew 18:21–22; Luke 17:3–4)?

12. When faced with the command to continually forgive others, Jesus' disciples asked Jesus to increase their faith (Luke 17:5–6). Why is faith necessary if you are to forgive others?

13. How did Jesus respond when the disciples asked him to increase their faith (Luke 17:6)? How is this encouraging to you?

 For You and God

Look back at what you wrote in the "For You Alone" section regarding your "mountains." You also may have written something under question 5 in the "For You and Others" section. Choose one of your mountains. Pray and read Scripture to try to determine God's will regarding this mountain. Then believe (exercise faith) and pray (take action) that God will answer your call for help.

If there is someone you haven't forgiven, confess it as sin and, in faith, leave the one who hurt you in God's hands. If your bitterness has robbed you of the enjoyment of life, seek God's healing by giving him your resentment. Going through these steps to healing will increase the power available to you in prayer. Go to him. He longs to show you his love and heal you and powerfully answer your prayers.

For You and Your Kids

Preschool–Elementary

Ask your kids, "Who has the power?" You probably won't be surprised by their answers. Some will know you want them to say "God." Others will quickly think of some action hero, like Spiderman or Superman. Explain to them that the *real* power is in God—power that is available to them in prayer.

Middle–High School

Talk to your children about the turmoil that is a part of life as a middle and high schooler. Let them talk to you. Listen as they reveal the turbulence they face daily in themselves and in their world. Be sure to let them know that they can tap into great power in prayer to overcome the temptations and anger and difficulties that this age brings.

All Ages

Remind your child that a complete faith is made up of belief and action. Explain that it doesn't take huge faith for prayers to be answered. God will honor the smallest person's smallest faith and use it to accomplish miracles.

session 4

where's the burden?

 For You Alone

True or False:

_____ I sometimes feel a strong urge to pray for someone.

_____ I have a friend or family member in such dire need that only direct intervention from God will help.

_____ I have certain people in need for whom I pray on a regular basis.

_____ I am sometimes so overwhelmed in prayer by a sense of identification with someone that I actually cry.

_____ I sometimes have a continual thought that motivates me to pray intensely for someone's need.

_____ I sometimes sense a heaviness or burden as I pray for someone.

Did you answer "True" to any of these statements? If so, then you are involved in intercession—praying for others. Anytime you pray for someone, whether you are asking God to bless them, to provide for them, or to meet a specific need, you are acting as an intercessor.

Intercession can be physically, emotionally, and spiritually draining. It can be a burden. But it can also be incredibly rewarding to see God powerfully at work and to be involved alongside God as an intercessor.

> *We must never wait until we feel like praying before we will pray for others. Prayer is like any other work; we may not feel like working, but once we have been at it for a bit, we begin to feel like working. . . . In the same way, our prayer muscles need to be limbered up a bit and once the blood-flow of intercession begins, we will find that we feel like praying. We need not worry that this work will take up too much of our time. . . . It is not prayer in addition to work, but prayer simultaneous with work.*
>
> RICHARD FOSTER, *CELEBRATION OF DISCIPLINE*

 ## For You and God's Word

Read Exodus 32. Moses had been up on the mountain with God for forty days and forty nights (Exodus 24:18). The people felt that God, as well as Moses, had abandoned them. But rather than turn to God, they turned to idols.

1. Has someone you know ever felt abandoned by God? Did he or she turn to someone other than God for help? Think about this person's situation. How could you pray for him or her?

2. God told Moses to leave him alone so he could destroy the people (verse 10). What did Moses do instead (verse 11)?

3. How far did Moses go in interceding for the people of Israel (verse 32)?

What does this action tell you about Moses' love for Israel? His burden for them in prayer?

4. What did Moses ask God to do (verses 12–13)? Why would Moses do this?

How did God respond to Moses' pleas (verse 14)?

God is almighty, and his power is unlimited. God is sovereign, and he can do as he pleases. But because God is gracious and merciful, he uses the prayers of his people—*your* prayers—to accomplish his plan and purposes.

For You and Others

As you begin, have a member of your group summarize the events of Israel's rebellion in Exodus 32. Then read Exodus 33:1–34:10 together and answer the following questions.

1. The people had broken their covenant with God. What was a consequence of the broken covenant (Exodus 33:3)?

2. How did the people respond to God's decision (verse 4)? Why?

3. Where did God meet with Moses (verses 7–9)?

4. How did God speak to Moses (verse 11)? How was this unusual?

5. For whom did Moses intercede in verses 12-13? Why?

6. What three things did Moses ask for (verses 13, 15-16, 18)?

7. How did God respond to Moses' three requests (verses 14, 17, 19)? Why did he respond (verse 17)?

8. In Exodus 34:5-7 God revealed himself to Moses as he had promised. See if you can list seven things Moses discovered about God's character (verses 6-7) in that revelation.

What was Moses' response to God's revelation (verse 8)?

How has God revealed himself to you?

9. Name a specific way God has responded when you interceded for someone in need.

10. Have you ever interceded for yourself? What was your need? How did God answer? How did you thank God for his answer to your prayer?

For You and God

Moses saved God's people from annihilation through his inter-cession (Psalm 106:19–23). Abraham did the same for Lot (Genesis 18:20–33). Job interceded for his less-than-helpful friends (Job 42:7–9). Jesus interceded for Simon Peter (Luke 22:31–32), for his disci-ples (John 17:6–19), for future believers (John 17:20–26), and for sinners while he was dying on the cross (Luke 23:33–34). And Jesus lives now to continually intercede for us at the Father's side (Romans 8:34).

Spend some time quietly contemplating persons you know who are in need of prayer. Ask God to give you a special burden, a spe-cial drive, to pray for these people. Then ask him to meet their needs. Allow the Spirit to use you to change lives, to meet needs, and to glorify God through intercession.

> *An intercessor means one who is in such vital contact with God and with his fellow men that he is like a live wire closing the gap between the saving power of God and the sinful men who have been cut off from that power.*
>
> HANNAH HURNARD, *GOD TRANSMITTERS*

 ## For You and Your Kids

Preschool–Elementary

Ask your children to name someone who needs a friend or is having a difficult time. If they sense another child's need or pain, encourage them to pray for that child. In order to motivate your chil-dren to pray for others, consider building a prayer journal of some kind together. Maybe you'd want to get a notebook and paste in pic-tures of the people for whom they're praying. Be sure to record with them not only the need and the prayer, but also how God answers.

Middle–High School

Ask your children of this age how you can pray for them and for their friends. Point out situations with their friends that may indi-cate a need for prayer. As a parent you can model a compassionate intercession for your children and their friends—an intercession that will build bridges between you during these often difficult years.

All Ages

Your children can be powerful intercessors as they pray for their friends and family members. Express your belief in their role as intercessors by asking them to pray for you (this is a two-way road to blessing). Be sure to share answers to prayer as a means of building up their faith.

session 5

where's the battle?

For You Alone

Look up each of these Scripture verses and record the many ways you're in a battle with Satan:

2 Corinthians 2:10-11 _____

2 Corinthians 11:3 _____

1 Thessalonians 2:18_____

1 Thessalonians 3:5_____

1 Timothy 3:6 _____

2 Timothy 2:25-26 _____

Revelation 12:10_____

We're in a battle, folks! It's not something to take lightly. Nor is it something to try to ignore. Satan's schemes are very real. He'd like nothing better than to find you vulnerable to his attacks, temptations, and deceptions. And he'd like nothing less than to find you strong and confident of your position as victor over him in Jesus Christ. The battles Satan chooses to pick with believers quickly affect the attitude and effectiveness of their prayer lives.

> *You wonder what to do when you feel attacked on all sides by seemingly irresistible forces, waves that cover you and want to sweep you off your feet. . . . What are you to do? Make the conscious choice to move the attention of your anxious heart away from these waves and direct it to the One who walks on them.*
>
> HENRI NOUWEN, *THE INNER VOICE OF LOVE*

 ## For You and God's Word

Second Corinthians 10:3–5 addresses the issue of spiritual battles that take place in the believer's mind. Examine this passage closely and answer the following questions.

1. Verses 3 and 4 clearly express the truth that spiritual conflicts cannot be dealt with by human will or material means. Name a spiritual battle you are fighting right now. (If you're not comfortable writing it down, simply bring it to mind.) For example, you may be battling unbelief, pride, lust, envy, hypocrisy, wounds from the past, anger, bitterness, vengefulness, or addiction. According to verse 4, what types of weapons are available to you in order to fight your battle?

2. Look up these verses and record what these weapons might look like.

2 Corinthians 12:10 _____

2 Timothy 4:16-17 _____

James 4:7b-8a _____

James 4:10 _____

A "stronghold" (verse 4) is "a fortified place; a place of security or survival" *(Webster's)*. A stronghold can start out as a means of protection but can proceed to become a dominating and negative force in your life. It can begin as a means of security but then become a prison.

3. What good things are you depending on that could become negative strongholds in your life? Think in terms of relationships, activities, and so forth.

4. How have you tried to break free of any stronghold in your life? Did you find freedom? If not, why do you think you were unable to break free (verse 3)?

5. Verse 5 gives a battle plan for destroying spiritual strongholds. List the three parts of this battle plan.

6. What does it mean to "demolish arguments" (verse 5) against God in your life?

   Where can you gain the wisdom and knowledge to do this (Colossians 2:2–3; 2 Timothy 3:16–17)?

7. How can you overcome "every pretension" (verse 5) that sets itself up against God in your life (James 4:10)? Pretensions can be such things as pride in your own ability and knowledge or rationalizations about your sin.

8. How can you "take captive every thought to make it obedient to Christ" (verse 5; see Philippians 4:8)? These are not fleeting thoughts but recurring, persistent, unyielding thoughts that draw you away from Christ.

Now for the good news: You have "divine power to demolish strongholds" (verse 4). Praise God! You no longer need to depend on your own human strength and skill. Instead, you can rely on God and the spiritual weapons he has provided.

For You and Others

According to Ephesians 6:10–18, you have armor you can wear in order to protect yourself against the devil's weapons. The battle with him is one you can win! As a small group, read this passage and answer the following questions.

1. What is the command in verse 10?

2. What do you have to put on in order to obey this command (verse 11)? How would you go about putting it on? Is it purely a spiritual act, or is there more to it? Why or why not?

3. Against whom are you fighting (verses 11-12)?

4. What is the purpose of the armor (verse 13)?

5. How would you describe the "day of evil" (verse 13)?

   How is this day a present reality? A future reality?

6. Why is truth (verse 14) important in spiritual warfare (Psalm 40:11)?

7. Why would Satan want to keep you from knowing the truth (John 8:32)?

8. Why is righteousness (verse 14) important in spiritual warfare (Isaiah 58:8-9)?

Why does Satan want to keep you from knowing that you are righteous before God (Isaiah 45:24)?

How can you be sure you are righteous before God (Romans 3:22)?

9. Why is peace (verse 15) important in spiritual warfare (Philippians 4:7)?

In these frantic and troubled times, how or where can you find peace?

Why does Satan want to steal your peace (John 14:27)?

10. Why is faith (verse 16) important in spiritual warfare (1 John 5:4)?

Why does Satan want to attack your faith (James 1:6–8)?

11. Why is salvation (verse 17) important in spiritual warfare (Isaiah 12:2)?

Why does Satan want to rob you of the certainty of your salvation (Psalm 62:7)?

12. What is the "sword of the Spirit" (verse 17)?

Why does Satan want you to keep your sword in its sheath (Isaiah 55:11)?

13. What does it mean to "pray in the Spirit" (verse 18; see Romans 8:26–27)?

What "occasions" (verse 18) might cause you to pray in the Spirit?

14. How do you stay "alert" as a believer?

Why is it necessary to stay alert?

For You and God

Look back at the spiritual battles or strongholds you noted in "For You and God's Word." Here are some steps to take to find freedom from any strongholds Satan may have over your life:

- Recognize that you have a stronghold in your life, whether it is an attitude, belief, thought, or relationship.

- Confess (agree with God) that your stronghold is sin, and repent (turn away from it).

- Discern what lies, arguments, and rationalizations you have believed in order to protect your stronghold.

- Verbally renounce these lies and claim the truth of Scripture. For example, replace fear with courage, condemnation with forgiveness, and so forth. Read aloud Scripture verses that support the truth (for example, for courage, read Deuteronomy 31:6; for forgiveness in Christ, read Romans 8:1–2).

- Memorize pertinent Scriptures. "Resist the devil, and he will flee from you" (James 4:7). When you are aware of condemning, accusing, or tempting thoughts, respond verbally with truth from Scripture. Use the name of Jesus.

- Put on the armor of God. (See "For You and Others.")

Your battle against strongholds may be an extended one, but do not give up! Your freedom is worth the effort. God himself wants to be your stronghold (Psalm 144:2).

 For You and Your Kids

All Ages

Watch TV with your children specifically to discover together the lies of your culture. TV shows tell you that living together without marriage is not only okay, it's also fun; that most people are rather stupid; and that swift put-downs are an acceptable and hilarious form of communication. TV ads tell you that white teeth equal happiness, that the right clothes will bring the right people into your life, and that smelling good equals being good. Talk with your children about how Satan uses these lies to influence their thoughts and actions. Without causing fear, impress on them their need for protection against the attacks Satan carries out on their minds. Encourage them to ask for God's help and protection. Stress that God's power is stronger than Satan's. Assure your children of God's love for them and of his mighty power to protect them.

where's the answer?

For You Alone

Have you ever prayed long and hard, but received no answer? When your prayers seem to go unanswered, it's easy to become discouraged. Sometimes it takes time for the answer to come. There could be a number of reasons for the delay:

1. Complicated situations require perfect timing (Genesis 18:14; Romans 9:9).

2. God may need to change the heart or attitude of the person for whom you are praying (Jeremiah 24:7).

3. The situation may require more prayers (Revelation 5:8; 8:3–5).

4. God may be removing things from your life that interfere with your spiritual growth (John 15:2).

5. There may be a battle in the spiritual world that is hindering the answer from being given to you (Daniel 10:1–2, 12–14).

6. God may be testing your faith or developing perseverance in order to strengthen your faith (James 1:3–4).

> *When God seems to be taking his time to decide if he will answer our prayer or not, we should get on our knees and affirm what we know to be true: God is sovereign, and he truly has everything under control, despite all seeming evidence to the contrary.*
>
> JILL BRISCOE, *PRAYER THAT WORKS*

Identify things that may be blocking your answer, so you can respond properly to the situation. Match the response below to its proper numbered item above (answers are found at the end of this session).

_____ Pray the words of Scripture (and perhaps fast) as a means to overcome the enemy's plans.

_____ Be persistent in prayer, claiming God's promises and trusting God's timing as you wait for him to act.

_____ Seek others to pray in agreement with you as you wait for God to work.

_____ Pray for God's guidance in the life of the person for whom you are praying.

_____ Persevere, trusting that God is doing something deep in your spiritual life.

_____ Search your heart for areas of sin. Confess your sin to God.

 ## For You and God's Word

When your prayers seem to go unheard, something may be blocking the answer from coming. Look up the following passages and write a word or two describing a reason why prayer may not be answered.

Psalm 66:18 _____

Proverbs 21:13 _____

Matthew 5:23–24 _____

Mark 11:25 _____

James 1:6–7 _____

James 4:3 _____

1 Peter 3:7 _____

1 John 5:14 _____

> *Sin is an awful thing, and one of the most awful things about it is the way it hinders prayer, the way it severs the connection between us and the source of all grace and power and blessing. Anyone who would have power in prayer must be merciless in dealing with his own sins.*
>
> R. A. TORREY, *HOW TO PRAY*

Sometimes God answers *no* to our prayers. Jesus got a *no* answer to his prayer in the Garden of Gethsemane. But because Jesus was truly righteous, the answer was due to something other than sin in his life. Read Matthew 26:36–46 and answer the following questions to help you determine the reason for the *no* answer (hint: it's the only reason in the above list that is not a sin).

1. Jesus prepared for prayer by going off to a quiet place by himself (verse 36). He asked for prayer support (verse 38). He did not hide his emotion from those who were supporting him in prayer (verse 38) or from God the Father (Luke 22:44). What do Jesus' actions teach you about prayer?

2. What "cup" (verse 39) did Jesus want removed? Since Jesus knew the reason he had come to earth, why would he pray this prayer?

3. How was Jesus' first prayer (verse 29) different from his second (verse 42) and third (verse 44) prayers in this passage? What does this tell you about Jesus' struggle?

4. How did Jesus' attitude when leaving Gethsemane differ from his attitude when he came to the garden? What does it teach you about prayer?

5. Although Jesus was perfect, he struggled as he submitted his will to that of the Father. Even though the answers to Jesus' prayers were *no,* how did God respond (Luke 22:43; Hebrews 5:7)? What does it teach you about prayer?

When your prayers aren't answered, don't get discouraged. Don't believe Satan's lies that God doesn't hear, that God doesn't care, or that it's humiliating to keep coming back to God with the same prayer. Be persistent, check your motives, look for unconfessed sin in your life, evaluate your fellowship with God and your relationships with other people. And most important, determine God's will. How do you do it? You'll discover how in the "For You and Others" section.

> *I want to hear what God hears, don't you? God wants all of us to be so in touch with him that we are tuned in to heaven's wishes for earth.*
>
> JILL BRISCOE, *PRAYER THAT WORKS*

For You and Others

Discovering God's will is an all-important factor in effective praying. Read 1 Corinthians 2:10–16 together and go on to answer the following questions regarding God and his will.

1. Think of a time in your life when you didn't know what to do. Whose advice did you seek in order to determine God's will in the matter?

2. What is the first requirement for discerning God's will (Psalm 40:8)?

3. Who knows the deep things of God (verses 10–11)? To whom, then, should you turn when trying to determine God's will?

4. How does the Spirit guide you (verses 12–13)? What can you do to prepare yourself to receive the Spirit's guidance (Romans 12:2)?

5. What does the Spirit do with "the deep things of God" (verse 10) and the things Jesus taught (John 14:26)?

6. In view of this, what does it mean to have "the mind of Christ" (verse 16)?

What would the mind of Christ look like in a believer's life?

How would having the mind of Christ affect your prayer life?

7. According to the following verses, what is your goal in determining God's will?

John 5:30 _____

John 11:4 _____

Philippians 1:12 _____

8. Prayer involves listening to God (Ecclesiastes 5:1–2), as well as speaking to him. According to the following verses, what questions can you ask to test whether what you heard from God is his will?

Luke 24:32 _____

John 10:35 _____

Romans 12:2 _____

2 Corinthians 10:5 _____

James 3:17 _____

1 John 4:6 _____

9. Describe the confidence in prayer you can gain when you know and understand God's will (1 John 5:14–15).

> *It is through God's holy word, taken up and kept in the heart, the life, the will; and through God's Holy Spirit, accepted in His indwelling and leading, that we shall learn to know that our petitions are according to His will.*
>
> ANDREW MURRAY, WITH CHRIST IN THE SCHOOL OF PRAYER

For You and God

Going over the lessons learned in the six sessions, select the one discovery that has most influenced your prayer life. Describe here what God has taught you.

Here are some practical ideas you can use to incorporate your discovery into your prayer life:

- Set aside a quiet place where you can pray (a whole room or just a particular chair). Although you may use this place for other things, allow it to take on special meaning as a place where you come to meet God.

- If possible, use praise music (either a CD or your own singing) to worship God before you begin your prayer time. This will allow time for your spirit to grow sensitive to the Holy Spirit's leading.

- Use your body to express your emotions through different postures (bowing, kneeling, dancing).

- Use the Lord's Prayer (Matthew 6:9–13) as a model for prayer.

- Use a prayer journal, recording your requests and the answers received. By doing so, you will build your faith as you pay attention to God's answers to your prayers.

- Pray with others. Start a prayer group with a few other people.

- Pray Scripture. Pray God's words back to him as a powerful expression of his will.

- Surrender to the Holy Spirit's leading.

- Fall in love with Jesus.

- Pray! You learn to pray by praying.

For You and Your Kids

Preschool–Elementary

The next time your children question how to pray about a specific situation, ask them, "What would Jesus pray?" As they try to form an answer, together you can discover what God's will in the situation may be. Talk with them about the importance of praying for God's will and wanting God's will in their lives.

Middle–High School

The next time your children need to make a decision (big or small), pray with them about the issue. After they've determined a course of action, go through the list of questions in question 8 on page 71 to test whether the decision falls within God's will.

All Ages

Buy a small notebook to be used as the family "Prayer Notebook." Record each family member's prayer requests, noting the date of the request. You can do this formally at mealtimes or informally as prayers are prayed. Remember to leave spaces after each request so you can note the answers and the dates they were answered. Once a month go through the notebook together, praising God for his great faithfulness in answering prayer.

Answers to the "For You Alone" on page 66: 5, 1, 3, 2, 6, 4.

leader's notes

The following notations refer to the questions in the "For You and Others" in each Bible study session. The information included here is intended to give guidance to small group leaders.

session 1:
welcome to the throne room

Question 1. In the Old Testament, the Most Holy Place was the innermost sanctuary of the tabernacle (later the temple). Within the Most Holy Place was the ark of the covenant, which represented God's throne and his presence (Exodus 25:22; Leviticus 16:2; Revelation 11:19). When the high priest entered the Most Holy Place, he entered God's presence.

Question 2. Jesus is our perfect high priest. He ascended into heaven and sat down at the right hand of God (Hebrews 8:1; 10:12). Note that, although Old Testament priests stood to perform their service (Hebrews 10:11), Jesus *sat down* (Hebrews 10:12), because his work was done.

Question 3. Jesus' death paid the price for our sin (1 Peter 2:24), his resurrection gave us new life (1 Peter 1:3), and his ascension gave us access into God's presence (Hebrews 4:14–16).

Question 4. We can pray confidently, knowing that God hears our prayers because in Jesus Christ we are forgiven. We can pray at any time, knowing that we have unlimited access to God because Jesus is interceding for us.

Question 5. As the curtain of the temple was torn to open the way into the Most Holy Place, so Jesus' body was torn (his blood was shed) to open the way into the heavenly Most Holy Place, that is, into God's presence. You can now freely—and often—enter God's presence, always remembering what Jesus Christ did to make it possible.

Question 6.

Part 1: A sincere heart. God desires honesty in prayer, for he knows our hearts and understands all things.

Part 2: A full and devoted faith. "Without faith it is impossible to please God" (Hebrews 11:6). With the smallest faith, mountains can be moved.

Part 3: A heart sprinkled to cleanse it from a guilty conscience. Some history is helpful here. When the people of Israel accepted God's covenant after the exodus (Exodus 24:3–7), Moses "took the blood [from the animal sacrifices and] sprinkled it on the people" (Exodus 24:8). The blood signified cleansing from sin, which allowed the people to enter into the new covenant relationship with God. Jesus has cleansed us by his blood so that we may enter into a covenant relationship with God (Matthew 26:28). What a beautiful picture—Jesus sprinkling our hearts, cleansing us with his blood, in order to give us a new relationship with God!

Part 4: A body washed with pure water. As Aaron and his sons were to wash their hands and feet before entering the tabernacle (Exodus 30:19–20), so we cannot enter God's presence until our bodies are cleansed by "pure water." God himself has cleansed us from all our impurities through Jesus, the Living Water, and he has given us new hearts and new spirits through faith in his Son (Ezekiel 36:25–26).

Question 7. Our access to God is dependent on God's faithfulness, not on our own, so we have a vibrant and vital hope as we pray.

Question 9. Our access to God will inspire us to encourage others to seek God and love others.

Question 10. When we read Scripture together, pray together, express our own spiritual longing for God, share our answers to prayer, and model a walk with God that is full of joy and satisfaction, we will encourage others to seek God and desire a more intimate relationship with him.

Question 11. To come close to you also.

Question 12.

2 Corinthians 3:18: We will be transformed so we become more Christlike.

Philippians 3:10: We will know Christ, gain his power, and become more like him.

Colossians 2:2–3: We will gain encouragement and love and the riches of knowing God.

2 Peter 1:3: We will gain everything we need for life and for godliness.

session 2:
where's the passion?

Question 1. In order to have a solid relationship with God, you need to "remain" in Christ, that is, have an intimate union with him. Some practical things you can do to achieve this: be filled with "the Spirit of Christ" (Romans 8:9), fill your mind with Scripture, surrender your will to God, spend time in prayer, express your love for God through extended times of praise, be honest with God in all things, expect God to speak to you through his Word and Spirit, and make obedience a priority in your life.

Question 2. Remaining in Christ will produce (1) individual spiritual growth, that is, the fruit of the Spirit (Galatians 5:22–23), and (2) the fruit of "good deeds" (Hebrews 10:24; see also Ephesians 2:10).

Question 3. The two conditions for answered prayer: "you remain in me" and "my words remain in you."

Question 4. The metaphor of the vine points to the importance of a living and continual spiritual union with Christ ("remain in me") in order to live a healthy, fruitful Christian life — one in which we know, believe, and obey Jesus' teachings, that is, his "words" (verse 7).

Question 5. Answered prayer glorifies God. Prayer is not a means to accomplish our own goals, plans, and expectations. Prayer is our cooperation with God in accomplishing *God's* plan and purposes.

Question 6. The purpose of prayer is to glorify God and to transform us into his fruitful disciples.

Question 7. Jesus compares his love for us with the Father's love for him.

Question 8. Obedience is the key to remaining in Jesus' love.

Question 9. Our obedience will produce real and lasting joy in our lives.

Question 10. Jesus was referring to his coming death. That someone would lay down his life for a friend is remarkable, but Jesus died for us when we were still his enemies (Romans 5:7–8). This was a demonstration of God's great love for us.

Question 11. We are now God's friends instead of his servants, recipients of a new relationship of intimacy, knowledge, and love. And our relationships with others are now defined by love instead of by some other baser emotion(s). Jesus' great love for us is the basis of our relationship with God, and it fuels our love for others.

Question 12. In verse 7 the condition for answered prayer is that we *remain in Christ.* Here in verse 16 the condition is that *we bear fruit.* The two are connected: Those who remain in Christ, who maintain an intimate relationship with him, will be fruit bearers and will see prayers answered. Also, the answers to prayer themselves can be seen as fruit, so praying believers bear the fruit of answered prayer.

Question 13. We are to love each other. Remember, this isn't a command to *feel* loving; it's a command to *be* loving and to *do* loving acts.

session 3:
where's the power?

Question 1. As Hebrews 11:1 declares, "Now faith is being sure of what we hope for and certain of what we do not see." Faith is not a mental exercise, nor is it based on intellect (Luke 10:21). Faith is not simply *affirmed* knowledge; it is a revelation that is *experienced* (1 Samuel 3:7). Faith is a gift (Ephesians 2:8–9) that proves itself through deeds (James 2:14–20). It grows through use (2 Corinthians 10:15; 2 Thessalonians 1:3).

Question 2. Doubt undermines faith. It causes us to be "double-minded" (James 1:8) and results in instability in life as well as in unanswered prayer.

Question 3. Satan does not want us to grow in faith. He does not want us to be effective in prayer, for when we pray, he is defeated. Doubt accomplishes the work of Satan.

Question 4. (1) Recognize your need for greater faith. (2) Exercise your "small" faith (Luke 17:6). (3) Read the Scriptures (Romans 10:17). (4) Pray. (5) Read about others' answers to prayer. (6) Keep a journal of prayer requests and answers to prayer. (7) Praise God for the "little" answers. (8) Depend on the Holy Spirit. (9) Be willing to take risks. (10) Obey when you sense the Spirit's leading. (11) Spend time with godly mentors. (12) Listen to praise music. (13) Attend a Bible study. (14) Memorize Scripture.

Question 6. God is the all-powerful Creator of the universe. He can do anything, including removing any obstacle about which you've been praying. However, there are times when he has other things in mind. Faithful, believing prayer will include room for God to accomplish his perfect will (Matthew 6:10).

Question 7. Faith is made complete by action (James 2:17, 22). Believing (faith) with the heart is joined to commanding (action) with the mouth (Romans 10:10) to form a whole, complete faith.

Question 9. God commands us to forgive others.

Question 10. When we refuse to forgive, our hearts begin to grow bitter and cold. We hold on to unforgiveness—either as a weapon or out of a false sense of security or protection. As we continue to cherish unforgiveness (sin) in our hearts, God will not listen to our prayers (Psalm 66:18).

Question 11. All the way! Jesus leaves no room for us to say, "*This time* I don't have to forgive!" When we forgive others, we leave revenge in God's hands (Romans 12:19) and trust God to protect us rather than using our unwillingness to forgive as a fortress against further injury.

Question 12. Luke 17:5–6 is framed by verses on forgiveness as an example of faith. We often need to make a choice regarding forgiveness when our feelings are not in agreement with what we know to be God's will (or God's *command* in this case). It takes faith to let go of the hurt and believe in God's ability to deal with the one who hurt us.

session 4:
where's the burden?

Question 1. God would send an angel to go with the people, but he would not personally go with them or live among them.

Question 2. They responded by mourning. They had experienced God's presence at Mount Sinai (Exodus 19:9–19) and were no longer satisfied with less than God's personal presence in their midst.

Question 3. At a tent Moses pitched outside the camp. This "tent of meeting" was not where God lived; Joshua lived there (Exodus 33:11). God only came to the entrance of the tent in order to meet with Moses (Exodus 33:9).

Question 4. God spoke to Moses as one friend speaking to another—a beautiful expression of their close relationship. At this time in history, God revealed himself so intimately to only a chosen few.

Question 5. Moses prayed for himself. Given the fact that God was not going to accompany the Israelites, Moses needed God's touch—his favor and teaching—in a special way.

Question 6. (1) "Teach me your ways" (Exodus 33:13); (2) "Go with us" (Exodus 33:16); (3) "Show me your glory" (Exodus 33:18). All of these requests struck at the heart of the issue: God's revelation of himself through his presence among his people.

Question 7. God's presence and his gift of rest would be with Moses (Exodus 33:14); God's presence would go with the people (Exodus 33:15–17); God would reveal himself to Moses as the God of goodness, mercy, and compassion (Exodus 33:19). God granted Moses' request for the people because he was pleased with Moses (Exodus 33:17). Because of God's favor toward Moses, Moses' intercession for the people was effective.

Question 8. God is compassionate, gracious, slow to anger, loving, faithful, forgiving, and just. In response to God's revelation, Moses bowed in worship and pleaded for God's presence among the people. In spite of their sin—even because of their sin—Moses asked God to dwell among his people in the tabernacle.

session 5:
where's the battle?

Question 1. "Be strong in the Lord and in his mighty power" (Ephesians 6:10). It is not in our own strength or ability that we engage in spiritual warfare. If we did so, we would surely be defeated. Jesus Christ has already triumphed over Satan and his demons (Colossians 2:15), so we engage in spiritual warfare from a position of victory.

Question 2. We have to put on "the full armor of God," which is a spiritual, not a physical, act. However, we can dress ourselves with God's armor *in our mind,* piece by piece, in order to increase our awareness of the effective weapons we've been given to use against Satan.

Question 3. We are not fighting against other people in spiritual warfare. Satan would like us to be deceived into thinking this is so, but it is not. We are fighting against Satan and his demons.

Question 4. The armor helps us stand against the attacks of Satan.

Question 5. The day of evil is any day in which we are engaged in battle with Satan. Satan would like to have us think this is a day that is only in the future. There *is* a future sense to it, when he will battle once and for all with Jesus—and lose. But there is a present tense to it also, experienced in the daily battle we wage against Satan, in small and big ways, as he tempts us to turn away from Jesus and the truths of the gospel.

Question 6. Jesus is truth (John 14:6), the gospel is the word of truth (Colossians 1:5), and the Holy Spirit guides us into truth (John 16:13). Truth protects us (Psalm 40:11). Truth sets us free (John 8:32). Satan wants us to remain in the bondage of his lies. When we engage in spiritual warfare prayer, we pray the truths of Scripture to defend ourselves against Satan, who is the "father of lies" (John 8:44).

Question 8. Jesus Christ is our righteousness (1 Corinthians 1:30). When we have faith in him, his righteousness is credited to us (Romans 4:23–24); he's on our side. Christ's righteousness and our righteousness in him are our protection against Satan. Satan knows that being righteous before God brings strength against him! In spiritual warfare, we can pray with quiet confidence (Isaiah 32:17) as we stand against the accusations of Satan, our enemy (Romans 8:33–34).

Our assurance of righteousness does not come from any sense of *feeling* righteous but from the stated *fact* of our righteousness, which is promised to all who believe (Romans 3:22).

Question 9. Jesus is our peace (Ephesians 2:13–14). Through faith in him we have peace with God (Romans 5:1), which gives us great hope and removes fear. Satan wants us to be fearful and emptied of all hope. He knows that when we find peace in God, we won't be afraid of Satan or his attacks. The peace we have as we trust in Jesus (Romans 15:13) gives us confidence to overcome the enemy through Christ's power (1 John 4:4).

Question 10. Our faith in Jesus Christ "overcomes the world" (1 John 5:4), that is, the evil in the world (Satan and his demons). Satan's goal is to cause us to doubt, which makes us ineffective and "unstable" (James 1:8), not only in spiritual warfare, but also as we live as Christ-followers every day. "Through faith [we] are shielded by God's power" (1 Peter 1:5) as we stand against the enemy.

Question 11. Jesus is the source of our eternal salvation (Acts 4:12; Hebrews 5:9). Because we trust in God's promise of salvation, we can also trust in his faithfulness to keep us blameless (1 Thessalonians 5:24) and to bring our salvation to completion (Philippians 1:6). Satan wants to shake our trust in God and God's ability to protect us. But God is our salvation and stronghold (Isaiah 26:1). We need never be afraid. We can find refuge in him in the midst of all of our spiritual battles.

Question 12. The "sword of the Spirit" is the Word of God, the Bible. If Satan can keep us from speaking the truth of God's Word, he can weaken our ability to defeat him. With Jesus as our example

(Matthew 4:1–11), we speak out the truths of Scripture in spiritual warfare prayer, for the words of Scripture cut through darkness, "dividing soul and spirit, joints and marrow" (Hebrews 4:12).

Question 13. Our prayers must not come from our own attitudes, emotions, or wisdom. As we submit to Jesus and surrender to the leading of the Holy Spirit, as we immerse ourselves in God's Word, we begin to pray in the Spirit. Almost any life circumstance can be an occasion for praying in the Spirit, but especially in those situations when our hearts groan with the weight of our prayers or when our minds simply don't know how to pray.

session 6:
where's the answer?

Question 1. Be sure to stress that there's nothing wrong with seeking godly guidance from other believers, friends, family members, or wise counselors. But our primary course of action should be taking our concerns to God in prayer.

Question 2. A sincere desire to follow it.

Question 3. The Holy Spirit knows all God's thoughts and will lead us into all truth (John 16:13) and show us God's will.

Question 4. The Spirit helps us understand the thoughts and ways of God. He may use the Scriptures to remind us of things Jesus taught. He may also use our spiritual experiences to help us apply to our lives what we have learned from Jesus. If we want to receive the Spirit's guidance, we can resolve that we will no longer be drawn into or influenced by the culture in which we live. Instead, we will turn our minds and hearts to Jesus and his teachings. Only then will our hearts and minds be prepared to receive guidance from the Spirit.

Question 5. The Spirit *reveals* the deep things and Jesus' teachings to our minds and hearts, which then become a part of who we are as believers.

Question 6. As we allow the Holy Spirit to teach us and guide us, our minds become tuned to his ways rather than the ways of our human nature or the ways of the world in which we live. We are being wonderfully "transformed" (Romans 12:2). We will begin to understand what it means to have "the mind of Christ" — which will become evident in all aspects of a believer's life. Certain actions and behaviors will be absent (Galatians 5:19–21), while others will be present and obvious (Galatians 5:22–25). In our times of prayer, the Spirit imparts to our spirit the mind of Christ, so we can discern God's will and receive answers to our prayers.

Question 7. John 5:30 — to please God; John 11:4 — to glorify God; Philippians 1:12 — to advance the gospel.

Question 8.

Luke 24:32: Did my heart burn within me, that is, did I sense agreement in my spirit? Did I sense an inner "aha" of agreement in my spirit?

John 10:35: Does what you heard from God or what you've determined to be God's will agree with the whole counsel of Scripture? If it contradicts Scripture, it is not from God.

Romans 12:2: Was your mind fixed on Christ at the time you heard from God or believe you determined God's will?

2 Corinthians 10:5: Did you take captive every thought to make it obedient to Christ? Does it align with what you know to be true of Christ?

James 3:17: Does what you heard or determined fit the qualifications of "wisdom that comes from heaven"? Will it produce "good fruit"?

1 John 4:6: Did you hold up to the mirror of Christ's character what you heard or determined?

Question 9. Once we know we are praying in God's will, we can pray with confidence, knowing that we have what we ask for.

bibliography

Arthur, Kay. *Lord, Teach Me to Pray in 28 Days.* Eugene, Ore.: Harvest House, 1995.

Bounds, E. M. *The Essentials of Prayer.* Grand Rapids: Baker, 1991.

Duewel, Wesley L. *Let God Guide You Daily.* Grand Rapids: Zondervan, 1988.

_____. *Mighty Prevailing Prayer.* Grand Rapids: Zondervan, 1990.

Flynn, Leslie B. *The Master's Plan of Prayer.* Grand Rapids: Kregel, 1995.

Kelly, Douglas F., with Caroline S. Kelly. *If God Already Knows, Why Pray?* Fearn, Scotland: Christian Focus Publications, 1995.

Kraft, Charles H. *I Give You Authority.* Grand Rapids: Chosen Books, 1997.

Matthews, Victor M. "Spiritual Warfare: A Biblical and Balanced View." 1992

Moore, Beth. *Breaking Free: Making Liberty in Christ a Reality in Life.* Nashville: LifeWay Press, 1999.

Murray, Andrew. *With Christ in the School of Prayer.* New Kensington, Pa.: Whitaker House, 1981.

Nee, Watchman. *Let Us Pray.* Richmond, Va.: Christian Fellowship Publishers, 1977.

Omartian, Stormie. *The Power of a Praying Parent.* Eugene, Ore.: Harvest House, 1995.

Pratt, Richard L., Jr. *Pray with Your Eyes Open.* Phillipsburg, N.J.: P & R Publishing, 1987.

Virkler, Mark, and Patti Virkler. *Communion with God: Study Guide.* Shippensburg, Pa.: Destiny Image, 1983.

A Mom's Ordinary Day

Finding Joy in All You Are

Jean E. Syswerda, General Editor
Written by Jean E. Syswerda

A Bible study series addressing the unique needs of moms

The demands of parenting can make you forget who you are besides Mom.
Dig into this Bible study and rediscover yourself as a whole person: wife,
friend, family member, beautiful person, and, most of all, believer. *Finding
Joy in All You Are* will help you discover more about yourself—a unique
creation of God—and how to make your life one of purpose, balance, and
beauty. Beauty? Yes. You may not have a perfect nose or be the Martha
Stewart of your neighborhood, but you're still breathtakingly beautiful to
God. He knows you completely, loves you best, and wants to show you
who you really are. That's worth celebrating!

The eight Bible studies in this series help women discover God's wisdom
on how to be the best mothers, women, and disciples they can be. Each
study contains six sessions divided into five flexible portions: For You
Alone, For You and God's Word, For You and Others, For You and God,
and For You and Your Kids. The last section helps moms share each
week's nugget of truth with their children.

Softcover
ISBN: 0-310-24712-8

Pick up a copy at your favorite bookstore!

ZONDERVAN™

GRAND RAPIDS, MICHIGAN 49530 USA
WWW.ZONDERVAN.COM

A Mom's Ordinary Day

Gaining and Being a Friend

Jean E. Syswerda, General Editor
Written by Jean E. Syswerda

A Bible study series addressing the unique needs of moms

No matter where you are in your life as a mom—buried in Cheerios and dirty diapers, or running the family schedule like a well-oiled machine—you need your friends. In many ways, your girlfriends are key kindred spirits, and it's their support and companionship that often gets you through the day. This Bible study explores friendship from a variety of angles, giving examples of several biblical people who were good friends, bosom buddies, soul mates. You'll examine these friendships as well as individual Scripture verses on the ups and downs of having and being a friend. Most of all, you'll learn the value of deepening your companionship with God, the one who created you to give and receive the gift of friendship.

The eight Bible studies in this series help women discover God's wisdom on how to be the best mothers, women, and disciples they can be. Each study contains six sessions divided into five flexible portions: For You Alone, For You and God's Word, For You and Others, For You and God, and For You and Your Kids. The last section helps moms share each week's nugget of truth with their children.

Softcover
ISBN: 0-310-24713-6

Pick up a copy at your favorite bookstore!

ZONDERVAN™

GRAND RAPIDS, MICHIGAN 49530 USA

WWW.ZONDERVAN.COM

A Mom's Ordinary Day

Growing Strong with God

Jean E. Syswerda, General Editor
Written by Jean E. Syswerda

A Bible study series addressing the unique needs of moms

Do you fret about what you're not instead of considering who you are in Christ? Spiritual strength doesn't come from building up your spiritual muscles. It comes from learning to rely on God's strength instead of your own, from recognizing your weaknesses and then leaning on him when you're feeling fragile. Delve into this study and discover your true source of strength. Grow strong in prayer, the Word, fellowship, and worship—and next time you're overwhelmed with whatever life has to throw at you, you'll be astonished at the power and vigor you have in God. As you work your way through this study, you'll meet God, and you'll find spiritual strength for each day.

The eight Bible studies in this series help women discover God's wisdom on how to be the best mothers, women, and disciples they can be. Each study contains six sessions divided into five flexible portions: For You Alone, For You and God's Word, For You and Others, For You and God, and For You and Your Kids. The last section helps moms share each week's nugget of truth with their children.

Softcover
ISBN: 0-310-24714-4

Pick up a copy at your favorite bookstore!

GRAND RAPIDS, MICHIGAN 49530 USA

WWW.ZONDERVAN.COM

A Mom's Ordinary Day

Mothering without Guilt

Jean E. Syswerda, General Editor
Written by Sharon Hersh

A Bible study series addressing the unique needs of moms

Motherhood and guilt go together like peanut butter and jelly. You feel guilty for not making organic baby food, not keeping up with your scrapbook . . . and don't forget your cluttered house. Does it ever end?

Yes, starting now. This study confronts guilt head-on. It will set your heart free to love, laugh, create, and cuddle, and to play and pray with your children. You'll meet new mentors—biblical women who model the possibilities of guilt-free mothering. As you confront your own guilt, be it over real failures or unrealistic expectations, you will find wonderful opportunities to connect with God. His love banishes all guilt and guides you into freedom in motherhood and all of life.

The eight Bible studies in this series help women discover God's wisdom on how to be the best mothers, women, and disciples they can be. Each study contains six sessions divided into five flexible portions: For You Alone, For You and God's Word, For You and Others, For You and God, and For You and Your Kids. The last section helps moms share each week's nugget of truth with their children.

Softcover
ISBN: 0-310-24715-2

Pick up a copy at your favorite bookstore!

ZONDERVAN™

GRAND RAPIDS, MICHIGAN 49530 USA

WWW.ZONDERVAN.COM

A Mom's Ordinary Day

Making Praise a Priority

Jean E. Syswerda, General Editor
Written by Ruth DeJager

**A Bible study series addressing
the unique needs of moms**

Dishes. Laundry. Nose-wiping and boo-boo kisses. The life of a mom
stretches out in predictable pattern of housework and nurturing. This Bible
study will inspire you to look up from your daily work and celebrate God's
presence, to become more aware of his nearness, power, and availability
to you. Let this study challenge you to raise your hands in praise and worship rather than to wring them in boredom and apathy. Start using your
voice to sing songs of praise rather than to grumble or complain. When
you make praise a priority, you will gain a fresh perspective on the chal-
lenges you face, and you will set a new and upbeat tone for your home.

The eight Bible studies in this series help women discover God's wisdom
on how to be the best mothers, women, and disciples they can be. Each
study contains six sessions divided into five flexible portions: For You
Alone, For You and God's Word, For You and Others, For You and God,
and For You and Your Kids. The last section helps moms share each
week's nugget of truth with their children.

Softcover
ISBN: 0-310-24716-0

Pick up a copy at your favorite bookstore!

GRAND RAPIDS, MICHIGAN 49530 USA

WWW.ZONDERVAN.COM

A Mom's Ordinary Day

Managing Your Time

Jean E. Syswerda, General Editor
Written by Erin Healy

A Bible study series addressing the unique needs of moms

What? You're too busy? Such is the life of a devoted mom—spending your day doing good things for your family, your community, and the Lord. But is your day so packed you have no time for reflection or for noticing God in the unexpected or for experiencing the joy he has built into your work as a mom, wife, and woman? Delve into this Bible study and discover the vision and purpose God has for you in the order of your days. Find out how to manage your time around that which is truly important, not just that which is good. Learn how God's generous wisdom will help you use all of your time for his glory, while taking care not to waste one precious minute.

The eight Bible studies in this series help women discover God's wisdom on how to be the best mothers, women, and disciples they can be. Each study contains six sessions divided into five flexible portions: For You Alone, For You and God's Word, For You and Others, For You and God, and For You and Your Kids. The last section helps moms share each week's nugget of truth with their children.

Softcover
ISBN: 0-310-24717-9

Pick up a copy at your favorite bookstore!

GRAND RAPIDS, MICHIGAN 49530 USA

WWW.ZONDERVAN.COM

A Mom's Ordinary Day

Winning over Worry

Jean E. Syswerda, General Editor
Written by Jean E. Syswerda

**A Bible study series addressing
the unique needs of moms**

Your kids. When you look at them, your heart swells with love—but sometimes with fear. Imagining the danger and horrors out there in the world just pierces a mom's heart. Worry can take away your breath, your confidence, your faith. It can even debilitate you and make you ineffective as a parent. Yet worry can be controlled. Find out how this crushing emotion can be confronted and defeated through solutions found in God's Word. Discover the peace God offers his children, and begin to win the battle over a worry-filled way of life. Learn to wield the power of prayer—your most potent weapon against fear. With help from God and his Word, you can replace worry with confident trust as you surrender to his will.

The eight Bible studies in this series help women discover God's wisdom on how to be the best mothers, women, and disciples they can be. Each study contains six sessions divided into five flexible portions: For You Alone, For You and God's Word, For You and Others, For You and God, and For You and Your Kids. The last section helps moms share each week's nugget of truth with their children.

Softcover
ISBN: 0-310-24719-5

Pick up a copy at your favorite bookstore!

GRAND RAPIDS, MICHIGAN 49530 USA

WWW.ZONDERVAN.COM